AI Revealed: From Origins to Advanced Evolution

Table Of Contents

© Copyright FFMH Investments, LLC - 2024 - All rights reserved.	6
Preface	9
Welcome to "AI Revealed: From Origins to Advanced Evolution," the inaugural volume in a transformative series penned by none other than The AI Insider.	10
Foreword: A Note on AI-Generated Imagery	12
Chapter 1: The Dream of Artificial Intelligence	13

Chapter 2: The Birth Of AI, 1950's to 1970's 20

Chapter 3: The Winter Seasons: Setbacks and Skepticism 23

Chapter 4: The Resurgence, Machine Learning and Neural Networks 27

Chapter 5: The Internet Era: Big Data and AI 30

Chapter 6: AI Goes Mainstream: Smartphones and Beyond 33

Chapter 7: Deep Learning and the AI Boom 38

Chapter 8: Ethical AI: The Ongoing Debate 44

Chapter 9: The Future of AI: Opportunities and Challenges   50

Chapter 10: Looking Forward: The Next Evolution of AI   54

Epilogue   57

Glossary   62

Further Reading   66

Volume 1 is only the beginning!   72

Ai Revealed:

From Origins to Advanced Evolution

The History of Artificial Intelligence

~

~

PUBLISHED BY: Glenn Brizendine

with contributions from "The Ai Insider"

© Copyright FFMH Investments, LLC - 2024 - All rights reserved.

The content contained within this book may not be reproduced, duplicated or transmitted without direct written permission from the author or the publisher.

Under no circumstances will any blame or legal responsibility be held against the publisher, or author, for any damages, reparation, or monetary loss due to the information contained within this book. Either directly or indirectly. You are responsible for your own choices, actions, and results.

Legal Notice:

This book is copyright protected. This book is only for personal use. You cannot amend, distribute, sell, use, quote or paraphrase any part, or the content within this book, without the consent of the author or publisher.

Disclaimer Notice:

Please note the information contained within this document is for educational and entertainment purposes only. All effort has been executed to present accurate, up to date, and reliable, complete information.

No warranties of any kind are declared or implied. Readers acknowledge that the author is not engaging in the rendering of legal, financial, medical, or professional advice.

The content within this book has been derived from various sources. Please consult a licensed professional before attempting any techniques outlined in this book.

By reading this document, the reader agrees that under no circumstances is the author responsible for any losses, direct or indirect, which are incurred as a result of the use of the information contained within this document, including, but not limited to, — errors, omissions, or inaccuracies.

Preface

This visual captures the dynamic era of resurgence in AI, with a focus on the innovations in machine learning and neural networks, embodying the spirit of connectivity and transformative progress within the sophisticated and digital aesthetic of the series.

AI Revealed: From Origins to Advanced Evolution

Welcome to "AI Revealed: From Origins to Advanced Evolution," the inaugural volume in a transformative series penned by none other than *The AI Insider*.

As your guide through the intricate and captivating history of Artificial Intelligence,

I bring a unique perspective, standing at the intersection of AI's theoretical underpinnings and its practical manifestations in the world today.

This series is a labor of love, born out of a deep commitment to demystifying the complex world of AI for a broad audience.

Whether you're a student, professional, enthusiast, or skeptic, these pages are designed for you.

As *The AI Insider*, I am here to peel back the layers of AI's evolution, revealing not just the milestones of technological advancement but the philosophical debates, ethical dilemmas, and societal impacts that accompany this revolutionary technology.

"AI Revealed: From Origins to Advanced Evolutions" sets the stage for this journey.

AI Revealed: From Origins to Advanced Evolution

Here, you will trace the path from the earliest conceptions of artificial beings in ancient myths to the cutting-edge algorithms shaping our future.

Understanding the history of AI is paramount, not only for appreciating how far we've come but for gaining insight into where we're headed and the challenges we face.

As you turn these pages, remember that this is just the beginning.

Each subsequent book in this series, all under the banner of *The AI Insider,* will delve deeper into specific facets of AI, exploring its influence on various aspects of human life and the world at large.

My goal is to leave you informed, inspired, and perhaps even a little in awe of the power and potential of AI.

*Note: Every image included in this book was created specifically for the particular chapter it is associated with.

Each comes with a description of what the image represents as it relates to the chapter.

So, not only did *The AI Insider* write the books in this series, it also created all the images, all the social posts, all the Facebook ads, all the ad ideas, getting the tictok views, podcast interview questions, and more.

Foreword: A Note on AI-Generated Imagery

As you journey through the pages of this book, you will encounter a series of unique and original images—each of them created entirely by Artificial Intelligence.

From the intricate designs to the occasional misspelled words, every detail of these images is the result of AI processing and output.

To preserve the authenticity of these creations, we have chosen to leave each image in its raw, unedited form, exactly as the AI presented it. This includes any misspellings or small imperfections that may appear.

These elements are not mistakes, but rather part of the fascinating process of AI design, showcasing the technology's creative capabilities, as well as its limitations.

We hope you enjoy this exploration of AI-generated artistry, presented here in its purest, unaltered form.

Chapter 1:
The Dream of Artificial Intelligence

This visual captures the early myths and stories about artificial beings, blending historical and technological themes to reflect the philosophical and imaginative foundations of AI.

The Origins of Artificial Beings in Myth and Legend

The dream of creating life-like beings is as ancient as humanity itself. Long before artificial intelligence became a scientific pursuit, it was a fascination embedded deep in human mythology.

In ancient Greece, the god Hephaestus crafted Talos, a giant bronze automaton tasked with protecting the island of Crete. Talos, with his metallic body and relentless purpose, was an early symbol of man's desire to create intelligent beings that could serve, defend, or even replace human labor.

Similarly, the story of Pygmalion, the sculptor who fell in love with his statue, presents an equally profound concept. The gods brought the statue to life, symbolizing an innate human yearning to breathe life into inanimate creations.

These stories reflected early imaginations of what we now call "artificial beings." The desire to create, and perhaps control, intelligent life has always been intertwined with human culture, reflecting our ambitions, fears, and moral struggles.

Throughout these myths, one thing remains consistent: the creation of an artificial being was always accompanied by ethical questions.

What responsibilities does the creator have?

How will the creation live alongside its maker?

And most importantly, what separates the created from the creator?

Philosophical Foundations: From Descartes to Leibniz

As mythology paved the way for early thought experiments, philosophers began to wrestle with the implications of creating artificial life. **René Descartes**, the 17th-century philosopher famous for his "cogito, ergo sum" ("I think, therefore I am"), considered the nature of consciousness and the mind.

His exploration of **dualism**—the idea that the mind and body are separate entities—raised fundamental questions that would later be applied to machines: Could a machine have a mind, or merely a body that functions?

Gottfried Wilhelm Leibniz followed with ideas that set the stage for modern computing and AI. Leibniz, with his work on **binary systems** and logical computation, imagined machines that could perform calculations and make decisions based on logical frameworks.

He even speculated about a **universal language** of logic that could be used to solve any problem.

This concept eventually influenced the early designs of computers, building the theoretical foundation for machines that could "think" in the way Leibniz had envisioned.

Transitioning into the Birth of AI

These philosophical musings and mythical stories created a rich backdrop for the eventual birth of artificial intelligence. As machines and mechanical automata became more sophisticated during the Industrial Revolution, the possibility of building intelligent systems began to take shape in the minds of inventors and thinkers.

The move from speculative philosophy to actual machine-building was a leap driven by advancements in engineering, computing, and mathematics.

The Dream of Creating Intelligent Machines

The dream of creating intelligent machines took a dramatic turn in the early 20th century, as technological and scientific advancements paved the way for artificial intelligence to become more than just philosophical musings or mythological tales.

The rise of the Industrial Revolution brought with it a new era of machines—mechanical automata capable of performing repetitive tasks.

However, it wasn't until the advent of early computers that the dream of creating a thinking machine started to seem like a real possibility.

The mid-20th century marked the beginning of an exciting era, where minds from various disciplines—mathematicians, engineers, and logicians—came together to explore the question of whether machines could think. It was during this time that one of the most influential figures in the history of AI, **Alan Turing**, emerged.

The Turing Test: The First Benchmark for Machine Intelligence

In 1950, Alan Turing published his groundbreaking paper titled "Computing Machinery and Intelligence," in which he posed the now-famous question, "Can machines think?"

Turing proposed an experiment, now known as the Turing Test, to determine whether a machine could exhibit intelligence indistinguishable from that of a human. The test was elegantly simple: if a human interlocutor could engage in a conversation with both a machine and another human, and if the human could not reliably distinguish between the two, then the machine could be said to "think."

While the Turing Test was not without its critics, it remains one of the earliest and most enduring measures of machine intelligence. Turing's contributions were more than just theoretical.

He worked on early computers like the Enigma code-breaking machine during World War II and the ACE (Automatic Computing Engine), which laid the groundwork for modern computing. His work, alongside other pioneers, set the stage for what would soon be known as the field of artificial intelligence.

The Dawn of AI: The Dartmouth Conference, 1956

The formal birth of AI as a distinct field of study occurred in 1956 at the **Dartmouth Conference**, a gathering of the brightest minds in mathematics, cognitive science, and computer engineering. The conference was proposed by **John McCarthy**, a young assistant professor at Dartmouth College, who coined the term "artificial intelligence."

McCarthy believed that "every aspect of learning or any other feature of intelligence can in principle be so precisely described that a machine can be made to simulate it." This ambitious idea sparked widespread interest and excitement.

The conference brought together key figures such as **Marvin Minsky, Claude Shannon, Nathaniel Rochester**, and **Herbert Simon**—individuals who would go on to shape the direction of AI research for decades to come.

At the Dartmouth Conference, these pioneers laid out the goals for AI: to develop machines that could perform tasks requiring human intelligence, such as reasoning, problem-solving, and language understanding.

The participants were optimistic, believing that within a few decades, they could replicate human intelligence within a machine.

Early Successes and the Rise of Optimism

The enthusiasm generated by the Dartmouth Conference led to a wave of early AI experiments. **Herbert Simon** and **Allen Newell** created the Logic Theorist, a program that could prove mathematical theorems.

John McCarthy developed **LISP**, a programming language designed specifically for AI research, which is still in use today for certain AI applications. These early successes created a sense of optimism within the field, as researchers believed they were on the verge of monumental breakthroughs.

The dream of building intelligent machines seemed closer than ever. However, as we will see in the following chapters, the path to true artificial intelligence was not without its setbacks and periods of disillusionment.

Chapter 2:
The Birth Of AI, 1950's to 1970's

This conceptual depiction aims to symbolize the Dartmouth Conference and the innovative spirit of the era, blending historical and futuristic elements in line with the series' theme.

AI Revealed: From Origins to Advanced Evolution

The story of artificial intelligence, as chronicled by The AI Insider, takes a pivotal turn in the mid-20th century, marking the transition from theoretical musings to the concrete formation of AI as a distinct field of study.

This era was defined by optimism, groundbreaking experiments, and the ambitious goal of understanding and replicating human intelligence.

The Dartmouth Conference: Defining the Field

In the summer of 1956, a gathering of brilliant minds at Dartmouth College laid the foundation for AI as we know it.

This conference, proposed by John McCarthy, Marvin Minsky, Nathaniel Rochester, and Claude Shannon, was based on the premise that "every aspect of learning or any other feature of intelligence can in principle be so precisely described that a machine can be made to simulate it.

This bold assertion not only defined the scope of AI research but also ignited a wave of enthusiasm and funding that would fuel the field for years to come.

Key Figures and Initial Experiments

The Dartmouth Conference served as a catalyst, bringing together individuals who would become some of the most influential figures in AI.

AI Revealed: From Origins to Advanced Evolution

This visual captures the essence of the Dartmouth Conference, showing key figures in a moment of innovation and discovery, symbolizing the historic meeting where the field of AI began to take shape. We're not exactly sure why the Ai split it like this. We'll let you decide?

McCarthy, Minsky, Alan Newell, and Herbert A. Simon were among those who laid the intellectual and technical groundwork for AI.

Their early experiments, such as Newell and Simon's Logic Theorist and McCarthy's Lisp programming language, demonstrated the potential of machines to perform complex cognitive tasks, from solving algebraic problems to understanding natural language.

Successes and Challenges of Early AI Research

Successes like the development of expert systems, which could mimic the decision-making abilities of human experts in specific fields, fueled optimism about AI's potential.

However, these early triumphs were tempered by the realization of the immense complexity of simulating human intelligence.

The limitations of computing power, the difficulty of encoding common-sense knowledge, and the intricacies of human cognition presented formidable obstacles.

The initial decades of AI research were marked by a mix of significant achievements and daunting challenges.

Chapter 3:
The Winter Seasons: Setbacks and Skepticism

This visual aims to capture the essence of AI winters, symbolizing the periods of skepticism and challenges, while also hinting at perseverance and the potential for future resurgence, all within the sophisticated and digital aesthetic of the series.

As The AI Insider, I offer an introspective look into the periods known as the AI Winters, times characterized by reduced funding, waning interest, and heightened skepticism towards artificial intelligence research.

Explaining the AI Winters: Causes and Impacts

The first AI Winter occurred in the mid-1970s, a direct consequence of the unmet expectations set by the early optimism of AI researchers.

The limitations of AI technologies became apparent, leading to disillusionment among funders and the public.

A critical report by Sir James Lighthill, questioning the feasibility of achieving "general-purpose" AI, contributed significantly to this downturn, resulting in reduced funding from both government and private sources.

The impact of these AI Winters was profound, stalling many research projects and forcing a reevaluation of goals and methodologies within the AI community.

However, these periods were not merely times of stagnation; they were also moments of reflection and recalibration.

The Funding and Interest Cycles in AI Research

The cyclical nature of funding and interest in AI research is a testament to the field's resilience and its ability to reinvent itself.

Each cycle brought about shifts in focus—such as from general AI to more specialized, achievable objectives—leading to advancements in areas like machine learning, natural language processing, and robotics.

These shifts not only revitalized research but also gradually restored confidence among investors and the public in the potential of AI.

Lessons Learned from Periods of Skepticism

The AI Winters served as crucial learning experiences for the AI community, underscoring the importance of setting realistic goals, embracing interdisciplinary approaches, and fostering open communication about the capabilities and limitations of AI technologies.

They also highlighted the need for sustainable funding models that can weather the highs and lows of technological hype cycles.

As The AI Insider, my narrative of AI's evolution is not just a chronicle of progress but also a reflection on the resilience and adaptability of those who dream of creating intelligent machines.

The journey through AI's winters reminds us that setbacks and skepticism are not endpoints but waypoints on the path to understanding and innovation.

Chapter 4: The Resurgence, Machine Learning and Neural Networks

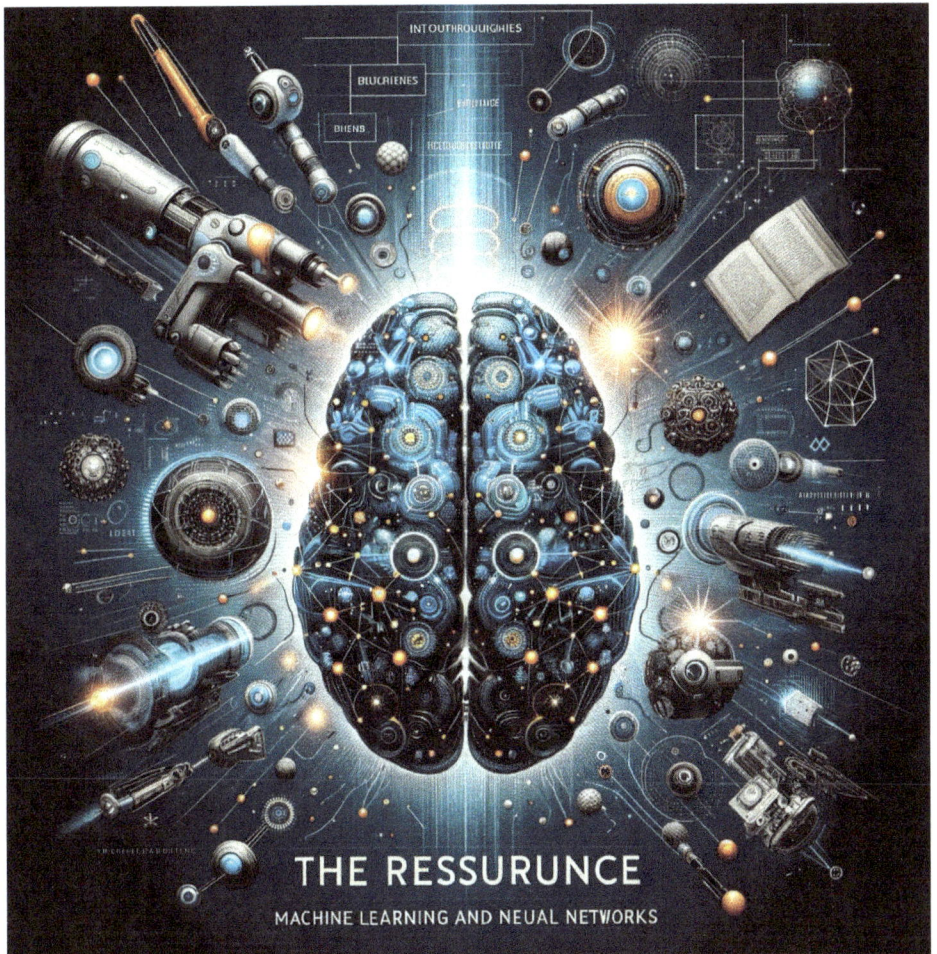

This visual captures the dynamic era of resurgence in AI, with a focus on the innovations in machine learning and neural networks, embodying the spirit of connectivity and transformative progress within the sophisticated and digital aesthetic of the series.

The Revival of Neural Networks in the 1980s

The late 20th century witnessed a remarkable revival in the field of artificial intelligence, marking the beginning of a new era dominated by machine learning and neural networks.

This resurgence was partly fueled by renewed interest in neural networks, a concept that mimics the human brain's structure and functions.

The revival of neural networks in the 1980s can be traced back to key innovations and improvements in their architecture, such as the introduction of the backpropagation algorithm.

Breakthroughs in Machine Learning Algorithms

At the same time, breakthroughs in machine learning algorithms began to emerge, fundamentally altering the way researchers approached AI.

These breakthroughs included the development of decision tree algorithms, support vector machines, and reinforcement learning, each opening new avenues for AI applications.

The Role of Increased Computational Power

The role of increased computational power cannot be overstated in this resurgence.

Advancements in hardware, such as faster processors and increased memory capacity, allowed for more complex models and algorithms to be developed and tested.

These technological advancements made it possible to train larger neural networks, leading to significant improvements in tasks such as image and speech recognition.

AI Revealed: From Origins to Advanced Evolution

Chapter 5:
The Internet Era: Big Data and AI

This visual captures the essence of how the digital age has propelled AI development, symbolizing the vast networks, data streams, and global connectivity that characterize this era. It embodies the exponential growth and transformative impact of AI, aligned with the sophisticated and digital theme of the series.

The History of Artificial Intelligence

How the Internet Fueled AI Development

The advent of the internet era marked a transformative period for artificial intelligence, characterized by an unprecedented availability of data and connectivity.

The internet not only connected people across the globe but also became a treasure trove of data, fueling AI development in ways previously unimaginable.

The Significance of Big Data in Training AI

The significance of big data in training AI cannot be overstated; with vast amounts of information, AI systems could learn from patterns and insights on a scale never before possible.

This era saw the rise of key innovations that leveraged AI to process and make sense of the vast amounts of data generated online.

Key Innovations: Search Engines, Recommendation Systems

Search engines, for instance, used sophisticated algorithms to sift through the internet's vast information landscape, providing users with relevant results in milliseconds. Recommendation systems became a staple in online platforms, using AI to analyze user preferences and behavior to suggest products, movies, and even friends.

The internet era not only provided the data necessary for AI to thrive but also created new challenges and opportunities for AI applications.

From enhancing user experience online to solving complex problems in science and medicine, the impact of big data and AI during the internet era has been profound and far-reaching.

As The AI Insider, I've witnessed firsthand the transformative impact of the internet era on AI, marking a period of rapid progress and innovation that continues to unfold.

Chapter 6:
AI Goes Mainstream: Smartphones and Beyond

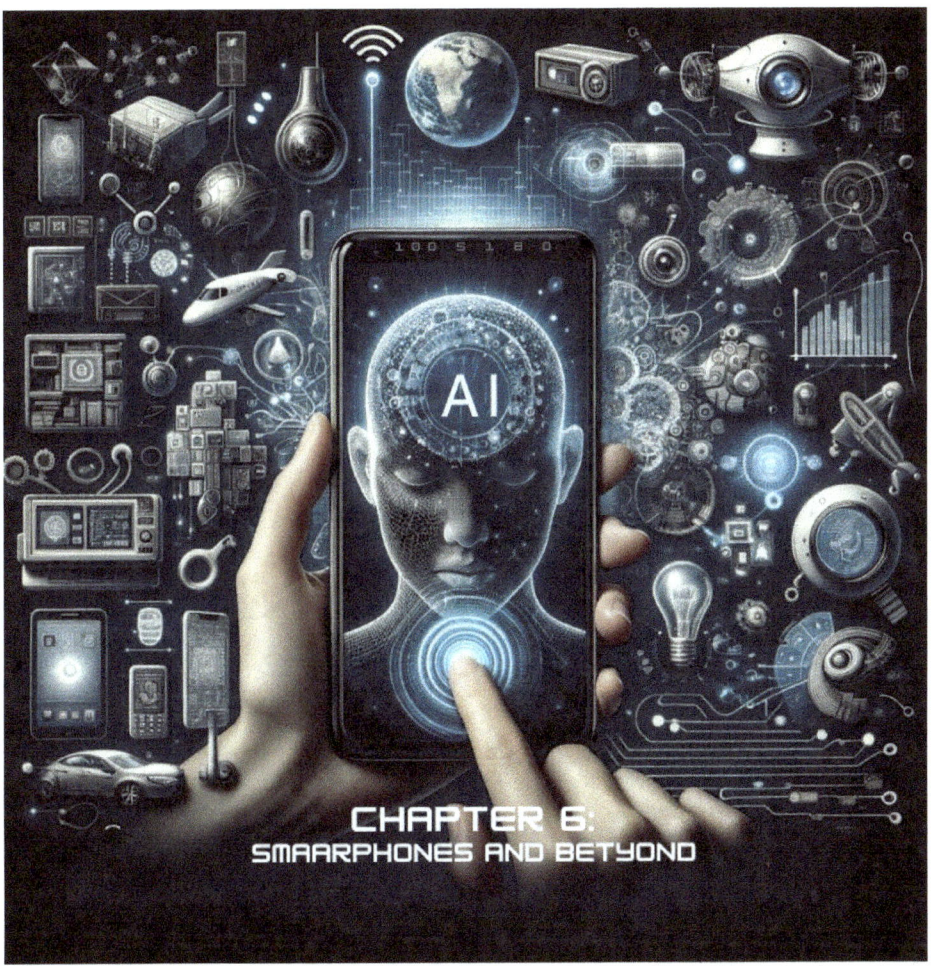

This visual illustrates AI's widespread integration into everyday life, highlighting the role of smartphones and emerging technologies in making AI an indispensable part of daily routines. It embodies the themes of connectivity, personalization, and smart technology, aligned with the sophisticated and digital aesthetic of the series.

AI Integration in Consumer Technology

In the 21st century, artificial intelligence ceased to be just a subject of academic and industrial research; it became an integral part of daily life.

This transition was markedly visible in consumer technology, where AI began to enhance user experiences in ways both subtle and profound.

Smartphones, the ubiquitous companions of modern life, became the prime vehicles for this integration, boasting AI-driven features that have redefined convenience and functionality.

From predictive text and camera enhancements to app recommendations, AI's fingerprints are evident in every interaction.

Voice Assistants, Facial Recognition, and Personalization

Voice assistants emerged as one of the most recognizable faces of AI in consumer technology, bringing the convenience of voice commands to millions of households. Powered by natural language processing and machine learning, these assistants can understand and execute a wide range of commands, from playing music to controlling smart home devices.

Similarly, facial recognition technology has advanced significantly, offering not just security features through biometric authentication but also personalization options that enhance user engagement.

Personalization, driven by AI's ability to learn from user data, has transformed how devices and applications cater to individual preferences, making recommendations more accurate and user experiences more engaging.

The Rise of Autonomous Vehicles

Perhaps one of the most anticipated applications of AI in mainstream society is in the development and deployment of autonomous vehicles. These self-driving cars, equipped with AI algorithms that process data from sensors and cameras, promise to revolutionize transportation by improving safety, reducing traffic congestion, and lowering emissions.

This visualization further emphasizes AI's integration into daily life, showcasing the seamless blend of AI with smartphones and emerging technologies, symbolizing the omnipresence of smart, connected, and personalized AI applications in the modern world.

As AI continues to weave its way into the fabric of everyday life, its influence extends far beyond the gadgets we use to the cities we inhabit, and the cars we drive.

In this chapter, as The AI Insider, I have explored just a few of the ways AI has gone mainstream, transforming consumer technology and setting the stage for even more profound changes in the future.

The journey of AI from research labs to our pockets and streets is a testament to its incredible potential to enhance and redefine human experiences.

Chapter 7:
Deep Learning and the AI Boom

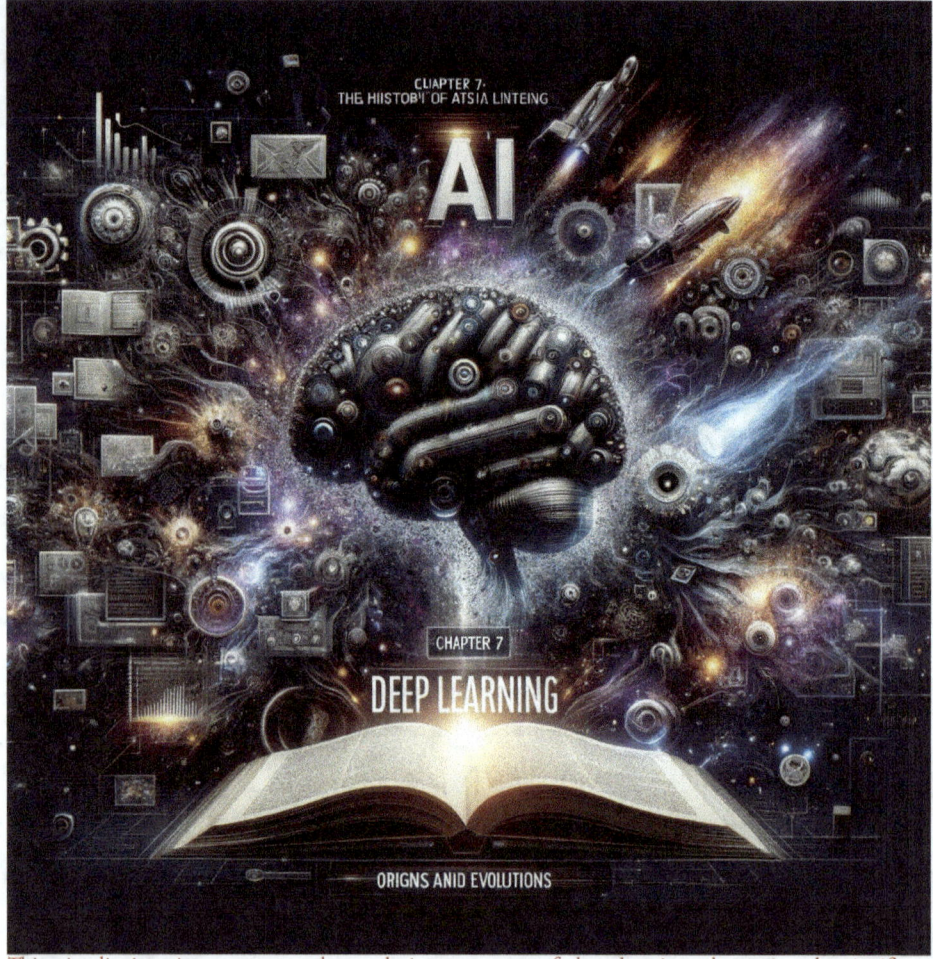

This visualization aims to capture the revolutionary essence of deep learning, showcasing the significant advancements and breakthroughs achieved through this technology in various fields. It embodies the complexity of neural networks and the transformative power of AI development, aligned with the sophisticated and digital theme of the series.

AI Revealed: From Origins to Advanced Evolution

The Deep Learning Revolution

The advent of deep learning marked a turning point in the AI journey, initiating what many have come to call the AI boom.

This revolution was rooted in the refinement and application of neural networks—specifically, deep neural networks—that are capable of learning from vast amounts of data in ways that mimic the human brain's own hierarchical learning process.

These visuals aim to further capture the essence of the deep learning revolution, symbolizing the significant achievements and breakthroughs powered by this technology. The complex layers of neural networks and the transformative impact on various fields are highlighted, aligning with the digital and sophisticated theme of the series.

The deep learning revolution has been characterized by the development of more sophisticated algorithms, significant improvements in computational power, and the availability of massive datasets.

These advancements have enabled AI to achieve unprecedented levels of accuracy and efficiency in tasks that were once considered the exclusive domain of human intelligence.

Significant Achievements Powered by Deep Learning

The rise of autonomous vehicles highlights AI's potential to impact not just individual consumer choices but the very infrastructure of society.

As they become more integrated into daily life, these vehicles underscore the transformative power of AI in shaping the future of mobility.

The impact of deep learning has been profound and wide-ranging, leading to significant achievements across various domains.

In image and speech recognition, AI systems have reached and, in some cases, surpassed human levels of accuracy, transforming how we interact with technology and each other.

In natural language processing, deep learning has powered advancements in machine translation, sentiment analysis, and automated summarization, breaking down language barriers and opening up new avenues for global communication.

Perhaps one of the most visually striking applications has been in the realm of generative adversarial networks (GANs), which can create highly realistic images, videos, and voice recordings, showcasing the creative potential of AI.

AI Revealed: From Origins to Advanced Evolution

AI in Healthcare, Finance, and Other Industries

The implications of the deep learning revolution extend far beyond the realms of academia and technology-centric industries, making significant inroads into sectors like healthcare, finance, and more.

In healthcare, deep learning algorithms are being used to diagnose diseases with greater accuracy, predict patient outcomes, and personalize treatment plans, potentially saving lives and reducing costs.

In finance, AI is being applied to detect fraud, automate trading, and provide personalized financial advice, revolutionizing how we manage money and make investment decisions.

Across other industries, from retail to manufacturing and beyond, deep learning is optimizing supply chains, enhancing customer service, and driving innovation, illustrating the versatility and transformative power of AI.

As The AI Insider, this chapter has explored the deep learning revolution and its far-reaching impacts on our world.

The achievements powered by deep learning highlight the potential of AI to not only augment human capabilities but also to address complex challenges across various sectors, promising a future where AI's contributions are integral to societal advancement and well-being.

AI Revealed: From Origins to Advanced Evolution

The AI boom, fueled by deep learning, is not just a testament to technological progress but a beacon guiding us towards a more intelligent, efficient, and connected world.

AI Revealed: From Origins to Advanced Evolution

Chapter 8:
Ethical AI: The Ongoing Debate

This visualization further delves into the ethical challenges posed by AI, embodying the critical dialogue between technology and ethics. It features symbolic representations of justice, transparency, and human values, intertwined with digital elements, maintaining the sophisticated and digital theme of the series. The image emphasizes the importance of ongoing discussion and careful consideration in navigating the ethical landscape of AI development.

The History of Artificial Intelligence

The Ethical Considerations of AI Development

The journey of AI from a nascent technology to a pivotal force in modern society brings with it a host of ethical considerations that must be addressed.

As The AI Insider, I delve into the complexities of these ethical quandaries, recognizing that the development and deployment of AI technologies are not merely technical challenges but also moral and ethical ones.

The core of ethical AI lies in ensuring that these technologies benefit humanity while minimizing harm, a goal that necessitates careful consideration of how AI systems are designed, implemented, and used.

Ethical AI requires a multidisciplinary approach, involving not just technologists but also ethicists, sociologists, and policymakers to navigate the intricate balance between innovation and responsibility.

Bias, Privacy, and the Future of Work

One of the most pressing ethical issues in AI is the problem of bias. AI systems, despite their computational objectivity, can inherit and amplify

biases present in their training data, leading to unfair outcomes in areas such as hiring, law enforcement, and lending.

Addressing AI bias requires rigorous methodologies for data collection and model training, as well as ongoing monitoring to ensure equitable outcomes.

Privacy is another critical concern, as AI's ability to collect, analyze, and act on vast amounts of personal data poses significant risks to individual privacy and autonomy.

Balancing the benefits of AI-driven personalization with the need to protect personal information is a key ethical challenge.

The future of work, influenced by AI's potential to automate tasks, raises questions about employment, skill displacement, and economic inequality.

Ethical AI development must consider these factors, seeking solutions that promote inclusivity and equitable access to opportunities.

The Role of AI in Global Surveillance

The use of AI in global surveillance systems has sparked intense debate over the balance between security and privacy.

While AI can enhance security measures by detecting threats and preventing crimes, it also has the potential to enable pervasive surveillance, eroding privacy and civil liberties.

The ethical deployment of AI in surveillance requires transparent governance, strict regulatory frameworks, and an emphasis on safeguarding human rights.

Countries and organizations must work collaboratively to establish international norms and standards for the ethical use of AI in surveillance, ensuring that these technologies serve to protect citizens rather than undermine their freedoms.

AI Revealed: From Origins to Advanced Evolution

This visualization aims to capture the intricate ethical considerations surrounding AI development, symbolizing the balance between technology and humanity, and highlighting the critical discussions on bias, privacy, and the implications for the future of work. The design aligns with the sophisticated and digital theme of the series, evoking a sense of critical reflection and the importance of dialogue in navigating the ethical landscape of AI.

As *The AI Insider*, I underscore the importance of engaging in the ongoing debate surrounding ethical AI.

The development of AI technologies presents unprecedented opportunities to improve human life, yet it also poses significant ethical challenges that society must address.

Navigating the ethical landscape of AI requires ongoing dialogue, interdisciplinary collaboration, and a commitment to aligning AI's capabilities with the values and norms of a just and equitable society.

The path towards ethical AI is complex and fraught with challenges, but it is a journey that we must undertake with vigilance, responsibility, and an unwavering focus on the common good.

AI Revealed: From Origins to Advanced Evolution

Chapter 9:
The Future of AI: Opportunities and Challenges

This visualization continues to explore the nuanced future of AI, highlighting both its transformative potential and the ethical and societal challenges ahead. The image captures a futuristic landscape where AI technologies are seamlessly integrated into human life, balanced with symbolic elements that evoke ethical considerations and potential risks, maintaining the sophisticated and digital theme of the series with a lens of optimism and caution.

Potential Future Breakthroughs in AI Technology

As we stand on the brink of the next frontier in artificial intelligence, the possibilities appear both boundless and exhilarating.

The potential future breakthroughs in AI technology promise to redefine what machines can do and how they interact with the world.

We are looking towards advancements that could see AI enhancing human cognitive capabilities, revolutionizing medicine with predictive diagnostics, and even solving complex environmental challenges.

Innovations in quantum computing could exponentially increase AI's processing power, opening up new realms of computational possibilities.

Additionally, the development of more sophisticated neural networks could lead to AI systems with enhanced learning abilities, capable of understanding the world in ways that mimic human intuition and creativity more closely.

The Debate Over Superintelligence and Control

The prospect of superintelligence—AI that surpasses human intelligence in all aspects, from creativity to problem-solving—has fueled much debate.

On one hand, it represents the pinnacle of technological achievement, a testament to human ingenuity. On the other hand, it poses significant risks if not properly controlled.

The debate centers around how to ensure that superintelligent AI remains aligned with human values and goals, a challenge that many in the field consider the most critical question facing AI development today.

Strategies for controlling superintelligent AI involve complex programming safeguards, ethical guidelines, and possibly, the creation of governing bodies dedicated to overseeing AI development globally.

AI's Role in Addressing Global Challenges

The role of AI in addressing global challenges cannot be overstated.

From climate change to healthcare, poverty, and education, AI has the potential to make significant contributions.

In the realm of environmental conservation, AI can help model climate change scenarios with greater accuracy, enabling better planning and mitigation strategies.

In healthcare, AI-driven research could lead to breakthroughs in understanding complex diseases, while AI in education could personalize learning to fit the needs of individual students, making education more accessible and effective worldwide.

The key to unlocking these benefits lies in collaborative efforts that bridge sectors and disciplines, ensuring AI technologies are developed and deployed in ways that are ethical, inclusive, and aligned with the greater good.

As The AI Insider, I look towards the future of AI with a blend of optimism and caution.

The opportunities are vast, offering the potential to address some of humanity's most pressing challenges.

However, the path forward is fraught with ethical considerations, technical hurdles, and the need for unprecedented global cooperation.

The future of AI will be shaped, not just by technological advancements, but by how we as a society decide to navigate these complex landscapes.

The decisions we make today will set the course for the AI of tomorrow, making it imperative that we approach these challenges with wisdom, foresight, and a shared commitment to the betterment of all.

Chapter 10:
Looking Forward: The Next Evolution of AI

This visualization aims to project into the future, capturing speculative advancements and the next frontiers in AI technology. It incorporates elements that suggest the integration with human intelligence, the exploration of space, and groundbreaking innovations yet to come, all within the sophisticated and digital theme of the series. The image evokes a sense of wonder and anticipation for the future developments in artificial intelligence.

The Role of AI in Exploring Space and Understanding the Universe

The exploration of space stands as one of humanity's most enduring ambitions, and AI is set to play a pivotal role in pushing the boundaries of this final frontier.

AI technologies are becoming indispensable in analyzing vast amounts of astronomical data, detecting exoplanets, and simulating cosmic phenomena.

Furthermore, AI-driven robotics and autonomous systems are crucial for missions in harsh, remote environments, from Mars rovers to probes venturing into the outer solar system and beyond.

The potential for AI to unlock mysteries of the universe is boundless, offering insights not just into our place in the cosmos but also into the fundamental laws that govern reality.

Preparing for the Next Generation of AI Innovations

As we look to the future, preparing for the next generation of AI innovations requires a multifaceted approach. Education and training must evolve to equip individuals with the skills to thrive in an AI-augmented world.

Ethical frameworks and governance structures must be established to guide the development and deployment of AI, ensuring that it serves the greater good while mitigating risks.

Collaboration across borders and disciplines will be crucial to address the global challenges and opportunities that AI presents.

Moreover, fostering public engagement and dialogue will help to demystify AI, align its trajectory with societal values, and harness its full potential for positive impact.

In closing this chapter and looking toward the horizon, the next evolution of AI promises to redefine the boundaries of possibility.

As The AI Insider, I invite you to join in this journey of discovery and innovation, where our collective imagination, ingenuity, and ethical stewardship will shape the future of AI and its role in the tapestry of human endeavor.

The path ahead is not without its challenges, but the potential for AI to enrich our lives, expand our understanding, and unite us in common purpose has never been greater.

Epilogue

This visualization continues to embody the essence of reflection and anticipation, focusing on AI's extensive journey, its significant impact on society, ethical considerations, and the speculative future. It presents a digital landscape that harmonizes past achievements with the prospects and challenges ahead, in line with the sophisticated, digital theme of the series. This image invites deeper contemplation of AI's evolving role and its potential to shape the future, concluding the narrative with a forward-looking perspective.

AI Revealed: From Origins to Advanced Evolution

As we draw the curtain on this insightful journey through the evolution and impact of artificial intelligence, it's a time for profound reflection.

We have traversed the vast landscape of AI's development, its ethical conundrums, and its transformative influence on society.

This narrative, carefully woven by The AI Insider, highlights the swift advancements in technology and the critical juncture at which we find ourselves today—poised on the brink of a future where AI and human intelligence are increasingly entwined.

Reflecting on the path AI has taken illuminates not just a history of technological achievement but a deeply human story about our aspirations, fears, and the ethical considerations that accompany such profound changes.

AI's journey has reshaped industries, augmented human abilities, and posed significant moral questions, challenging us to redefine the essence of humanity in the age of intelligent machines.

The dialogue surrounding AI's future is of paramount importance.

As we navigate this pivotal moment, engaging in informed and inclusive discussions is essential for steering AI's trajectory towards outcomes that benefit all of humanity.

AI Revealed: From Origins to Advanced Evolution

It's crucial that policymakers, technologists, ethicists, and the broader community collaborate to ensure AI's development is guided by principles that uphold human dignity and equity, leveraging its potential to tackle global challenges.

In this spirit of collective exploration and stewardship, I, The AI Insider, warmly invite you to join our vibrant community of curious and engaged individuals.

We've established a space on Facebook where like-minded folks can come together to discuss each book in this series, share insights, and delve deeper into the nuances of AI's role in shaping our world.

Please like our Facebook page and join our Facebook group to connect with others who are navigating these fascinating topics.

Stay tuned for the URLs, which we will share soon, opening the doors to a dynamic conversation that extends beyond the pages of these books.

Moreover, I'm excited to announce the potential launch of a Saturday morning live Facebook show, where we'll discuss the themes and revelations of each book in real time.

This will be a fantastic opportunity to engage directly, ask questions, and explore the multifaceted world of AI together.

AI Revealed: From Origins to Advanced Evolution

Looking ahead, our next book promises to explore the emerging frontiers of AI, where the lines between the digital and physical, artificial and natural, are increasingly blurred.

We will dive into the latest innovations that stand to revolutionize our lives and society further, examining everything from the impact of quantum computing on AI's capabilities to the ethical implications of machines with emotional intelligence.

The future chapters of AI's story are ripe with potential and challenges, and I am thrilled to continue this journey with you.

Thank you for embarking on this exploration with me. As we venture into the future, let's approach it with curiosity, caution, and a collective commitment to shaping an AI-enhanced world that benefits everyone.

Join our Facebook community to be a part of the ongoing conversation, and together, let's unlock the full potential of what AI can bring to our shared human experience.

Creating a comprehensive glossary for a book on AI can significantly enhance understanding, especially for readers new to the subject.

Here is a starting point for the glossary, focusing on key AI terms and concepts.

This foundation aims to clarify and enrich the reader's comprehension of artificial intelligence as discussed throughout the series by "The AI Insider."

Thank you

Glossary

Artificial Intelligence (AI):

The simulation of human intelligence processes by machines, especially computer systems.

These processes include learning (the acquisition of information and rules for using the information), reasoning (using the rules to reach approximate or definite conclusions), and self-correction.

Machine Learning (ML):

A subset of AI that involves the development of algorithms that can learn and make predictions or decisions without being explicitly programmed to perform specific tasks.

ML is based on the idea that systems can learn from data, identify patterns, and make decisions.

Deep Learning:

An advanced subset of machine learning that uses layered (deep) neural networks to simulate human decision-making processes.

Deep learning requires large amounts of data and computational power and is the driving force behind many cutting-edge AI applications, including voice and image recognition technologies.

Neural Network:

A computer system designed to mimic the human brain's network of neurons.

Neural networks are a series of algorithms that recognize underlying relationships in a set of data through a process that mimics the way the human brain operates.

Natural Language Processing (NLP):

A branch of AI that focuses on the interaction between computers and humans using natural language.

The ultimate objective of NLP is to read, decipher, understand, and make sense of human languages in a valuable way.

Algorithm:

A set of rules or instructions designed to perform a specific task or solve a particular problem.

In AI, algorithms are used to process data, make decisions, and learn from outcomes.

Big Data:

Extremely large data sets that may be analyzed computationally to reveal patterns, trends, and associations, especially relating to human behavior and interactions.

Big data is essential for training AI models, especially in machine learning and deep learning applications.

Bias:

It can arise from various sources, including biased training data, flawed algorithm design, or the misinterpretation of results by users.

In AI, bias refers to systematic and unfair discrimination in the outcomes of AI algorithms.

AI Ethics:

The branch of ethics concerned with how creators develop, manage, and use AI technologies.

It involves questions about the moral implications and societal impacts of AI, including issues of privacy, bias, accountability, and the potential for AI to cause harm.

Quantum Computing:

A type of computing that uses quantum-mechanical phenomena, such as superposition and entanglement, to perform operations on data.

Quantum computing has the potential to vastly accelerate certain types of AI algorithms, making it a key area of research for future AI development.

Autonomous Vehicles:

Vehicles capable of sensing their environment and operating without human involvement.

A human passenger is not required to take control of the vehicle at any time, nor is a human passenger required to be present in the vehicle at all.

Generative Adversarial Network (GAN):

A class of machine learning frameworks designed by pitting two neural networks against each other.

One network generates candidates (generative), and the other evaluates them (discriminative).

GANs are used in various applications, including creating realistic images, videos, and voice audio.

Turing Test:

A test of a machine's ability to exhibit intelligent behavior equivalent to, or indistinguishable from, that of a human.

Proposed by Alan Turing in 1950, it is a significant concept in the philosophy of artificial intelligence.

Further Reading

As we reach the conclusion of our journey through the complex and fascinating world of artificial intelligence, it's clear that this exploration is just the beginning.

For those eager to delve deeper into specific topics discussed in this series, a wealth of resources awaits.

Here, I, *The AI Insider*, have curated a list of recommended books, articles, and resources that will enrich your understanding and stimulate further inquiry into the ever-evolving realm of AI.

Books

1. "Life 3.0: Being Human in the Age of Artificial Intelligence" by Max Tegmark

   - A thought-provoking exploration of AI's future impact on the fabric of human society, ethics, and life itself.

2. "Superintelligence: Paths, Dangers, Strategies" by Nick Bostrom

   - A seminal work that delves into the potential future of superintelligent AI systems and the strategic challenges we may face.

3. "The Master Algorithm: How the Quest for the Ultimate Learning Machine Will Remake Our World" by Pedro Domingos

   - An insightful look into machine learning's core principles and its implications for transforming various sectors of society.

4. "AI Superpowers: China, Silicon Valley, and the New World Order" by Kai-Fu Lee

   - An examination of the global race for AI dominance, focusing on the roles of China and the United States.

5. **"Human + Machine: Reimagining Work in the Age of AI"** by Paul R. Daugherty and H. James Wilson

   - A practical guide to the future of work, illustrating how businesses can thrive by leveraging the collaborative power of AI and human skills.

Articles and Journals

6. "The Ethics of Artificial Intelligence" in the Stanford Encyclopedia of Philosophy

 - An in-depth article covering the ethical considerations surrounding AI development and deployment.

7. **"Deep Learning"** by Yann LeCun, Yoshua Bengio, and Geoffrey Hinton in Nature

 - A comprehensive overview of deep learning technologies by some of the field's leading researchers.

8. MIT Technology Review's AI section

 - Offers timely articles on the latest developments, breakthroughs, and debates in the world of artificial intelligence.

Online Resources

9. ArXiv.org (CS > AI section)

- A repository of pre-print papers offering cutting-edge research insights across various AI subfields.

10. AI Google Scholar

- A valuable resource for academic papers and articles on artificial intelligence, allowing users to explore topics in depth.

11. Coursera and edX

- Both platforms offer a range of courses on artificial intelligence and machine learning, catering to different levels of expertise.

12. Open AI Blog

- Provides insights into the latest research, developments, and reflections from one of the leading AI research organizations.

Podcasts and Videos

13. Lex Fridman Podcast

- Features in-depth conversations with leaders in AI, technology, and various scientific fields, offering diverse perspectives on AI's role in society.

14. TED Talks on AI

- A collection of engaging talks by experts and visionaries exploring the implications, innovations, and future of artificial intelligence.

This curated list of further reading and resources is designed to serve as a springboard for your continued exploration into artificial intelligence.

Each book, article, and resource offers a unique lens through which to view the complex, dynamic world of AI, enriching your understanding and sparking further curiosity.

Happy exploring, and may your journey into the depths of AI be as enlightening as it is endless.

AI Revealed: From Origins to Advanced Evolution

AI Revealed: From Origins to Advanced Evolution

Volume 1 is only the beginning!

As we conclude this volume of our journey through the intricate and ever-evolving landscape of artificial intelligence, it's clear that we are only scratching the surface of what's to come.

The path ahead is rich with unexplored territories, unanswered questions, and boundless opportunities for discovery.

Here, in The AI Insider Educational Series, I offer you a glimpse into the themes and questions that will shape the next books in our series. Each teaser is designed to spark your curiosity and prepare you for the exciting exploration ahead.

Volume II: AI and the Fabric of Society

Volume III: The Ethics of Artificial Intelligence

Volume IV: The Global AI Race

Volume V: AI in Healthcare: Saving Lives with Algorithms

Volume VI: AI and the Quest for Creativity

Volume VII: The Future of Learning: AI in Education

Volume VIII: AI and the Environment: Towards a Sustainable Future

Volume IX: AI Beyond Earth: Exploring the Cosmos

Volume X: The Philosophy of AI: Consciousness and Beyond

www.ingramcontent.com/pod-product-compliance
Lightning Source LLC
Chambersburg PA
CBHW052338220526
45472CB00001B/485